CONTENTS

About the Whole Foods Meal Prep Recipes in this Book

The Whole Foods Meal Prep recipes in this book are designed with real families in mind: the kind who want to eat real, whole foods, but also need to keep dinner quick, easy, and affordable.

Within these pages you'll find my very favorite Whole Foods Meal Prep recipes. They're the keepers that I turn to again and again, and here's why I think you'll love them, too:

Each Whole Foods Meal Prep recipe aims for:

● **Easy-to-find, affordable ingredients:** You won't find any expensive or unpronounceable ingredients here. While there are a few keys items you'll want to buy when you stock your whole foods compliant pantry, I make sure they get used over and over in other recipes, so you're not stuck with an ingredient you'll never use again. (I hate that!)

●**Kid-friendly, adaptable recipes:** My daughter and her friends are super picky eaters, so I always create recipes with them in mind. These Whole Foods Meal Prep recipes in this book are as simple as they can be while still being flavorful. Even better, each recipe says whether it's especially kid-friendly. Where possible, I included suggestions for how to adapt the recipe for both adult and kid taste buds. Remember, these recipes are designed to serve as templates for meal prep meals, so never hesitate to skip or substitute flavoring ingredients like spices or sauces if your kiddos don't like them!

● **7 Ingredient or Less recipes:**If you're like me and don't want to spend tons of time pulling ingredients from cabinets and measuring them, these Whole Foods Meal Prep recipes are for you! The recipes will point out if it's a 7 Ingredient or Less recipe (not including salt and pepper, of course). That way, you can easily turn to these recipes on nights when you really want to keep things simple. (Helloooo, Wednesday night soccer practice.)

● **20 Minutes or Less recipes:**The beauty of the whole foods meal prep lifestyle is that it saves you tons of time and stress on weeknights. But that doesn't mean you should spend hours and hours in the kitchen on the weekend, either. That's why I've highlighted the recipes that are 20 Minutes or Less to cook, so you can quickly turn to those when you have less time for meal prep on the weekend.

Chapter 1: An Overview of the 30 Day Whole Foods Challenge

A 30 day Whole Foods challenge can mean many things, but most commonly it's considered to be a grain-free, dairy-free, legume-free, sugar-free diet that focuses on eating only natural, whole foods. You can do the diet for 30 days to reset your body, or you can stick with it indefinitely. At its core it is an elimination diet, meaning that it's designed to cut out foods that cause weight gain, decrease your energy, or which cause inflammation or food sensitivities in many people.

Oftentimes, we *think* we have no problem eating certain foods, but we're usually too busy, too distracted, or too out-of-tune with our bodies to notice that they're making us feel bloated, tired, or just heavy-feeling. By seeing how we feel when we cut out those foods for 30 days, we can finally—usually for the first time in our lives—see how our bodies feel when we fill them only with real, nourishing food.

What Not to Eat During the 30 Day Whole Foods Challenge

Grains

No pasta, bread, rice, corn, quinoa, barley, farro, wheat, and other grains.

Legumes

No beans, peas, lentils, chickpeas, peanuts, soy in any form, and other legumes.

Dairy products

No milk, cheese, yogurt, cream, butter and other dairy. Ghee (clarified butter) is compliant with most popular 30 day whole foods diets because it does not contain lactose.

Sugar

No stevia, artificial sweeteners, honey, maple syrup, agave, and others. Only fruit or fruit juice is okay as a sweetener.

Alcohol

No beer, wine, and liquor, either for drinking or cooking.

Additives

No MSG, carrageenan, nitrates, and any other non-food ingredients.

What to Eat During the 30 Day Whole Foods Challenge

The great news is that there are so many foods you CAN eat during your 30 Day Whole Foods challenge, and once you start adjusting to this new way of eating and seeing how amazing it makes you feel, you won't want to go back to your carb-loading, sweet tooth ways.

You can eat as much as you want of these compliant foods:

Compliant Foods:

> Meat
> Poultry
> Seafood
> Vegetables
> Eggs
> Potatoes (Potatoes are compliant because they're a whole food, but fries, chips, and any other deep-fried potatoes are excluded because they are often processed.)
> Fruit
> Nuts and seeds (excluding peanuts, which are a legume)
> Oils and ghee

The following are popular compliant ingredients:

Almond flour	Coconut Water
Almond milk	Coconut Aminos
Arrowroot Powder	Coffee
Bacon	Dates
Bean Sprouts	Flax Seed
Cacao	Fruit Juice
Canola Oil	Green Beans
Olive Oil	Hemp Seeds
Carob	Mustard
Chia	Nutritional Yeast
Citric Acid	Sunflower Oil
Coconut Flour	Snow Peas

Chapter 2: Guidelines for Buying Organic Produce and Whole Foods

Buying organic can be expensive, but we all want to feed our families the healthiest and safest fruits and vegetables. That's where the Dirty Dozen and Clean Fifteen come in.

Each year, the Environmental Working Group issues its Shopper's Guide to Pesticides in Produce, which ranks the pesticide contamination of popular fruits and vegetables. Rankings are based on data from more than 35,200 samples which are tested each year by the U.S. Department of Agriculture and the Food and Drug Administration.

The top 15 types of produce that have the least amount of pesticide residue are known as the Clean Fifteen, while the top 12 most contaminated fruits and vegetables are called the Dirty Dozen.

By knowing which fruits and vegetables contain more pesticides and which contain less, you can make more informed choices and stretch your grocery dollar further.

The Dirty Dozen

When possible, buy these organic.

1. Strawberries
2. Spinach
3. Nectarines
4. Apples
5. Peaches
6. Pears
7. Cherries
8. Grapes
9. Celery
10. Tomatoes
11. Sweet bell peppers
12. Potatoes
13.

The Clean Fifteen

These do not need to be bought organic.

1. Sweet Corn
2. Avocados
3. Pineapples
4. Cabbage
5. Onions
6. Sweet peas
7. Papayas
8. Asparagus
9. Mangos
10. Eggplant
11. Honeydew Melon
12. Kiwi
13. Cantaloupe
14. Cauliflower
15. Grapefruit

Chapter 3: Why Meal Prep?

What is Meal Prep?

Meal prep is exactly what it sounds like: planning and preparing a week of breakfasts, lunches, dinners, and snacks in advance so weeknight cooking angst becomes a thing of the past.

In theory, diets should be easy to follow. But when you get home from a long day of work and know you have a whole hour of chopping and cooking ahead of you, you'll end up going with that frozen pizza or fast-food burger more often than not. And when you've had a late night followed by a stressful morning, it's easy to give up on packing a healthy, balanced lunch in favor of the sandwich counter.

But with meal prep, suddenly, almost magically, the healthy, homemade meal becomes just as easy and appealing as the unhealthy, store-bought meal. After all, don't Fluffiest 4-Ingredient Pancakes, piping hot in just 2 minutes, sound better than cold cereal from a cup? And wouldn't you rather come home to meal-prepped Takeout Asian Salmon and Broccoli, ready for you in 2 minutes, than the oily, fattening equivalent you'd lose 30 minutes and $15+ for?

With meal prep, not only will you save hours of time each week, but you'll also save hundreds of dollars each month by buying affordable, whole food ingredients instead of overpriced, processed junk foods.

Just think: if you spend two hours on Sunday meal prepping instead of watching Netflix, you'll get to hit snooze one more time in the morning, skip the day-long angst over what to eat for dinner, and use the $20 you would have spent on takeout to buy yourself something you *really* want. (Personally, nothing motivates me like a new pair of shoes!)

Meal prep is a lifesaver for anyone on a diet, but it can especially change the game for families with kids and parents rushing off to school and work at the same time. Instead of giving your kid five dollars to buy a sodium-filled, nutrition-devoid school lunch, plan a healthy meal for your child on the weekend that's easy to put together on a weeknight. This ensures that you're in control of what your child is putting into his or her body *and* that you actually have time to talk to each other in the morning, instead of arguing over what goes in the lunch box!

Why Meal Prep Works

Meal prep is so effective because it redistributes your time. Even if you spend two hours on the weekend putting together dinners, you'll spend only 5-10 minutes each weeknight reheating and putting together your pre-prepped meal. Meal prep also uses efficiencies of scale to drastically reduce how long it takes to prep and cook—instead of pulling out your cutting board, collecting ingredients, washing ingredients, chopping, washing your cutting board, etc. every single night, you'll do it all only once on the weekend, saving you so much time and energy.

Even better, meal prep takes advantage of the times in the week when you have more energy—namely Saturday and Sunday—to do something productive, which can even be fun if you're not crunched for time and mentally drained from a long day. And on weekdays, when you just don't have the energy or the focus to put together a full meal, you'll be thanking yourself that dinner is done. Lastly, having a ready-to-go meal prep waiting for you at home eliminates the motivation to go out and buy a much less nutritionally beneficial meal that will cost you more.

If you're anything like me, you know that it's hard to be creative when you're stuck in a cooking rut and that holding yourself accountable to make healthy meals is easier said than done. I'm especially guilty of succumbing to mid-week stress-eating, and I've been known to eat way more than my body eats if something good is in front of me. That's why I love that meal prepping gives you a chance to try out new recipes and plan an exciting, delicious weekly menu for your family, all while keeping each serving to an appropriate portion-size. It also gives beginning-of-the-week, motivated You the power to make healthy choices for tired Thursday night You.

The power of meal prep is especially game-changing for families. Putting together meals that appeal to four or five different palates and preparing packed lunches for everyone rushing off to work or school requires a magical level of creativity, so being able to work everything out in advance not only saves time, but it gives you a chance to breathe during busy mornings. It also gets rid of the temptation to take hangry, whining kids to a fast food restaurant, because you know you already have a mostly-done meal waiting at home.

It's especially important to meal prep on a whole foods diet. Because the whole foods diet is more restrictive of ingredients than other diets, the trap of fast food isn't just your run-of-the-mill unhealthy—it can also throw off your whole challenge and force you to start the 30 day countdown all over again.

That's why the whole foods diet is such a perfect fit for the meal prep lifestyle. Each perfectly portioned meal made up of healthy and delicious ingredients is exactly what you need to stick to your challenge, without all the hassle of putting together each meal one-by-one. By doing all the planning and prepping on the weekend, you'll always have a healthy and delicious whole foods meal ready to go in your refrigerator, no matter what else the week throws at you!

How Meal Prep Works

Meal prep may seem daunting at first; after all, it does require you to do most of a week's worth of planning, cooking, and packaging in one afternoon. However, there are ways to ease into the process without overwhelming yourself, and before you know it, you'll have your meal prep routine down to a science.

The very first time you meal prep, you might want to stick with familiar recipes. When people begin to meal prep in order to stick to a diet, they tend to expect themselves to put together unfamiliar dishes that comply with the diet's regulations. But there are often ways to update or improve dishes you make on a regular basis to comply with the diet without throwing you off of your cooking rhythm; just check out the substitutions section! This way, you'll know that your family will like what you're cooking, and putting the meal prep together won't add any additional stress.

After your first week of meal prep, you'll have a better sense of how to structure your meal prep sessions. Remember that it's highly encouraged to skip planning a few meals (maybe you want to eat out 1-2 nights per week?) and to repurpose leftovers. You'll get burned out if you try to cook three square meals a day from scratch, so this is the time to get creative and see how leftovers, no-recipe nights, and a little help from the store can round out your meal plan and make it feel manageable.

If you want more specific guidelines for getting started, here's a rough plan:

Step 1: Plan Your Meals

On a Saturday or Sunday–or whatever day is your least busy–sit down with a pad, pencil, and a few cookbooks (including this one!), and make your meal plan for the week.

Tips for Planning Dinner

At least 1-2 dinners should be favorites you could make with your eyes shut and which don't require a recipe, and 2-3 should be able to be thrown together at the last minute. Also try to choose dinners that share similar ingredients so that you can cook food in advance. For instance, decide on three chicken dishes and two vegetarian dishes, so that you can cook all the chicken in advance.

Tips for Planning Breakfast

Choose 2-3 make-ahead breakfast casseroles, egg muffins, or other recipes you could make on the weekend and reheat for the morning. But give yourself some flex space with breakfasts—some mornings grabbing a snack bag of almonds or a nut bar may be more realistic!

Tips for Planning Lunches

The key to making easy lunches is asking yourself: What can you reuse from dinner? Many of the recipes in this book can be doubled so you'll have leftovers for hot lunches for adults. Or you can add a compliant wrap, lettuce wrap, grain-free crackers, or other sides to make an easy lunch for a kid's lunch bag. If your dinner recipes don't transform into lunch as well as you'd like them, plan a few easy wrap options or soup options that could be packed in a thermos.

If someone in your family has very specific dietary restrictions, track down as many nonperishable options for their lunches as possible, such as snack packs of nuts, dried fruit, or jerky, so that you can purchase large amounts at a time at a discount.

Tips for Planning Snacks

My theory with snacks? Keep it simple. Finding snacks that everyone likes, such as boiled eggs, nut bars, or almond packets will give you the opportunity to buy in bulk or cook a large batch of those snacks in advance to throw into lunches at the last minute. Fresh fruit (such as raspberries, which are low-sugar and good for your whole foods diet) and vegetables (such as celery sticks and baby carrots) are also great to have on hand for snacks, because they require little more than a rinse and a plastic baggie from you.

Step 2: Make Your Grocery List and Do Your Shopping

Now that you have your meal plan, review all the recipes and meal outlines and write up your grocery list. If you or certain people in your household are following a whole foods diet, this is also the time to check that you have compliant versions of ingredients you may be used to relying on, like ketchup, mayo, dressings, sauces, etc. I recommend trying to do your grocery shopping one day and your prep another day, so that it feels even more manageable. But if that doesn't work with your schedule, then get it all done in one day—you'll feel so accomplished once you're done! Ideally, you'll have planned your dinners so there are some shared proteins and vegetables among them, so keep an eye out for deals for buying things like chicken, beef, long-lasting vegetables (like potatoes!), and eggs in large quantities. You'll save loads of money and time this way!

Step 3: Make Your Prep List and Execute

Before you do any prep, I recommend reading through your recipes and writing a list of things that can be done ahead of time. For instance, a typical list for my meal prep sessions might look like

> Chop 3 onions. Divide into 1 cup portions for Monday and Tuesday.
> Wash, chop, and bag broccoli for Monday dinner.
> Wash, chop, and bag carrots and celery.
> Make egg muffins and freeze.
> Cook and shred pork loin.
> Combine sauce ingredients for chicken.

As you'll see, sometimes you'll want to make a recipe all the way through and refrigerate or freeze it, and other times you'll want to prep the ingredients so they can easily be thrown together in the oven or your Instant Pot during the week. Whether you make a recipe all the way through or simply prep the components is up to you. All of the recipes in this book are designed to store well, so any of them can be completely made in advance and simply reheated when it's time to eat. But if you prefer certain items cooked fresh, or if you know you'll have more time on Wednesday than you will on Monday, you might prefer to simply prep and then cook fresh on the day of. Either way, you'll be saving yourself hours of chopping and prep time during the week, so even an impressive dinner will be a breeze to put together! If you want to adapt recipes you already know for your new whole foods meal prep lifestyle, it's important to figure out which foods last in the fridge and which need to be frozen, which vegetables can stay uncooked until the last minute, and which you can cook in advance to save time. You can often simply Google "does [ingredient] freeze/store well" to find a quick answer. Finding a grocery shopping guide, whether it is online or on a diet app, will also help you shape your meal planning around foods that comply with your family's specific diet and needs.

Every family is different, but taking a few minutes to learn about the best way to store the foods you most like will allow you to enter your meal-prepping sessions armed with everything you need to know to make healthy, wholesome, delicious meals in no time!

My Secret Weapon for Meal Prep

Just because you'll be spending almost no time in the kitchen on weeknights doesn't mean you should have to spend hours in the kitchen on weekends. We all love our weekends too much for that, right?

That's why the Instant Pot is my secret weapon for speedy meal prep. With the Instant Pot electric pressure cooker as your sidekick, you can drastically cut down on the amount of time you need to do your meal prep. You can have your Instant Pot quietly and quickly cooking your proteins or sides in less than half the time of a slow cooker or oven, all while you work on chopping vegetables and other prep work.

After experimenting with the Instant Pot electric pressure cooker for nearly a year, I've learned a few hacks that make the best use of this handy new appliance. I use these almost every single time I make a Whole Foods Meal Prep recipe, and they've saved me hundreds of hours in the kitchen, plus resulted in more flavorful meals.

1. Thicken the sauce, if you have the time.

Because the Instant Pot always needs to have about 1 cup of liquid in it to cook correctly, you'll get delicious broths and sauces with nearly every meal.

But sometimes, you might find that you have too much liquid after cooking, and that it's a bit thin. Sauté setting: to the rescue! If I have time, I'll often remove the food from the Instant Pot, leaving the sauce, and then set the pot on high heat on the Sauté setting. You can let it cook down as much as you want, or add a thickener to make it more like a gravy. A great Whole Foods compliant thickener is arrowroot powder, which you can find online or at specialty food stores.

> **To make an arrowroot powder thickener:**
> Combine 1 teaspoon arrowroot powder + 1 tablespoon water.
> Slowly whisk into the liquid and allow to cook until thickened.

2. Use the pocket of time during pressure cooking to make a side.

When I first start looking for Instant Pot recipes, it seemed like many of them had you first cook the protein, then empty the pot and cook a vegetable side. Yikes—I don't have time for that! If you don't either, here's what I suggest: get your Instant Pot recipe locked and loaded, then use the time during pressure cooking to quickly roast vegetables, spiralize your zucchini or carrots, microwave a few baked potatoes, or do whatever else is on your meal prep task list.

My favorite Whole Foods compliant side is a big tray of brussels sprouts, cauliflower, or broccoli, which I cook under the broiler instead of roasting, to save even more time.

To make quick and easy broiled vegetables:

Toss 1-inch pieces of any oven-friendly veg with olive oil, salt, and pepper.

Place under the broiler until crispy, watching carefully so they don't burn.

3. Taste your food before serving and add more salt and pepper, if necessary. We all like our food at different levels of saltiness and pepperiness, so please always take my measurements as a suggestion, not a rule! This is especially true of any Instant Pot recipes that you might be meal prepping, since you're often using broth as the steaming liquid. Different brands of broth have vastly different salt content, so if you're unsure how salty your broth might be, use less salt before pressure cooking. You can always add more salt and pepper once you open up the pot again!

Chapter 4: Whole Foods Compliant Pantry Staples

Whole Foods Compliant Homemade BBQ Sauce

Kid-Friendly

20 Minutes or Less

Makes 2 cups

Prep Time: 0 Minutes

Cook Time: 10 Minutes

½ cup unsweetened apple juice

¼ cup tomato paste

1 teaspoon garlic powder

1 teaspoon onion powder

1 teaspoon paprika

¼ teaspoon cayenne pepper (Or ½ teaspoon, if you like spicy BBQ sauce.)

½ teaspoon salt

2 tablespoons apple cider vinegar

Optional: 1 teaspoon liquid smoke

Select the Sauté setting on the Instant Pot. Add all of the ingredients and stir well. Allow to cook for at least 10 minutes, until thickened. Taste and adjust salt or spice level to your taste.

Note: This barbeque sauce will be less sweet than you might be used to, because it has no added sugar. To add more sweetness, you can puree 5 pitted dates in a food processor with a bit of water and incorporate into the sauce.

To store: Ladle the sauce into food-safe containers and store in the refrigerator for up to 5 days or in the freezer for up to 2 months.

Whole Foods Compliant Lemon Pepper Seasoning

Kid-Friendly

7 Ingredients or Less

20 Minutes or Less

Prep Time: 5 Minutes

Cook Time: 0 minutes

Ingredients

6 lemons, zested

2 teaspoons garlic powder

1 tablespoon freshly cracked black pepper

2 teaspoons salt

In a small bowl, combine all ingredients.

To store: Store in a tight-sealing container in the refrigerator and use on chicken, fish, potatoes, and vegetables.

Whole Foods Compliant Taco Seasoning

Kid-Friendly
7 Ingredients or Less
20 Minutes or Less
Prep Time: 2 Minutes
Cook Time: 0 minutes

Ingredients

2 tablespoons chili powder
1½ tablespoons ground cumin
2 teaspoons garlic powder
¼ teaspoon cayenne pepper, or to taste
1 teaspoon dried oregano
2 teaspoons salt
1 teaspoon black pepper

In a small bowl, combine all ingredients.

To store: Store in a tight-sealing container at room temperature and use on chicken, fish, meat, potatoes, and vegetables.

Whole Foods Compliant Italian Seasoning

Kid-Friendly
7 Ingredients or Less
20 Minutes or Less
Prep Time: 2 Minutes
Cook Time: 0 minutes

Ingredients

1 tablespoon garlic powder
½ tablespoon dried oregano
½ teaspoon crushed red pepper flakes
1 teaspoon dried basil
1 teaspoon dried thyme
1 teaspoon salt
1 teaspoon black pepper

In a small bowl, combine all ingredients.

You can also make a delicious Italian dressing by adding olive oil and apple cider vinegar to this seasoning and shaking well. This makes a healthy, additive-free, sugar-free Italian dressing that can be used to marinate chicken, fish, and pork or can be drizzled over roasted vegetables.

To store: Store in a tight-sealing container at room temperature and use on chicken, fish, meat, potatoes, and vegetables.

Whole Foods Compliant Indian Spice Mix

Kid-Friendly
7 Ingredients or Less
20 Minutes or Less
Prep Time: 2 Minutes
Cook Time: 0 minutes

Ingredients

2 tablespoons curry powder

2 tablespoons cumin

2 teaspoons turmeric

2 teaspoons ground coriander

1 teaspoon ground ginger

½ teaspoon cinnamon

In a small bowl, combine all ingredients.

To store: Store in a tight-sealing container at room temperature and use in curries or on chicken, fish, meat, potatoes, and vegetables.

Chapter 5: Whole Foods Meal Prep Egg Recipes

Instant Hard-Boiled and Soft-Boiled Eggs
Kid-Friendly

20 Minutes or Less

7 Ingredients or Less

Makes 2-12

Prep Time: 1 minute

Cook Time: 3-5 minutes

Ingredients

2-12 eggs (You can cook as many as fit in one layer in the pot.)

Directions

Place the Instant Pot trivet inside the pot. Arrange eggs in one layer on top of the trivet and add 1 cup of water to the pot.

Lock the lid and set the Pressure Release to Sealing. Select the Pressure Cook or Manual setting and set the cooking time to 5 minutes for hard-boiled eggs or 3 minutes for soft-boiled eggs at high pressure.

Once the timer goes off, use a kitchen towel or oven mitts to protect your hand and move the Pressure Release knob to Venting to perform a quick pressure release. Cool eggs under running water and peel.

To store: Allow to cool and store eggs in a microwave-safe container. Cut in half before reheating individually in the microwave in 30-second intervals or serve chilled. Eggs will keep up to 5 days in the refrigerator.

Ham and Green Onion Egg Cups

Kid-Friendly
7 Ingredients or Less
Serves 4
Prep Time: 5 minutes
Cook Time: 10-15 minutes

Ingredients

Oil spray (such as olive)
16 slices ham (check that it contains no sweeteners or non-compliant ingredients)
8 large eggs
2 green onions, sliced
Salt and pepper to taste

Directions

Preheat oven to 350 degrees. Grease a standard-size muffin tray with oil.

Line each muffin cup with two slices of ham. Crack an egg into each muffin cup and sprinkle with salt and pepper.

Bake for 10 minutes for a softer egg or 15 minutes for a hard-boiled egg. Top with green onions and serve warm.

To store: Allow to cool and store eggs cups in a microwave-safe container. Reheat individually in the microwave in 30-second intervals. Egg cups will keep 5 days in the refrigerator and up to 2 months in the freezer.

age and Broccoli Crustless Quiche

ndly

7 Ingredients or Less

Serves 8

Prep Time: 10 minutes

Cook Time: 30 minutes

Marle ½

Ingredients

1 tablespoon unsalted butter, divided

1 lb. ground pork sausage, sweet or spicy

½ cup broccoli florets, chopped in ½ in. pieces

1 green onion, thinly sliced

10 large eggs

¼ cup unsweetened unflavored almond milk

½ teaspoon garlic powder

¼ teaspoon salt

Pepper to taste

Directions

Preheat the oven to 375 degrees and grease a 9x13 baking dish with 1 teaspoon butter.

In a large skillet over medium-high heat, melt remaining 1 teaspoon butter. Add the ground sausage and brown, breaking it up into smaller pieces. Spread into the bottom of the baking dish and top with the broccoli florets and green onion.

In a medium bowl, lightly beat eggs, almond milk, garlic powder, salt, and pepper and pour into baking dish. Bake for 18-22 minutes, or until no longer soft in center.

To store: Let quiche cool then cut into 8 squares for a full breakfast or 16 squares for a snack. Wrap squares individually in aluminum foil and place in a resealable plastic bag. To reheat, remove from foil and heat in 30 second intervals in the microwave until warm. Quiche will keep 5 days in the refrigerator.

Fluffiest 4-Ingredient Pancakes

Kid-Friendly
7 Ingredients or Less
20 Minutes or Less
Serves 2 (4 small pancakes per serving)
Prep Time: 5 minutes
Cook Time: 10 minutes

Ingredients

2 large bananas
4 large eggs
1 teaspoon cinnamon
1 teaspoon vanilla extract
Pinch of salt
2 teaspoons coconut oil, divided

Directions

In a blender or mixer, mix together all ingredients except coconut oil until a smooth batter is formed.

In a large nonstick skillet over medium heat, melt 1 teaspoon coconut oil. Using a ladle, spoon half of the pancake batter into skillet, making 4 small rounds. Once each pancake begins to bubble, flip and cook another 1-2 minutes, until cooked through. Repeat with remaining 1 teaspoon of coconut oil and remaining batter.

If desired, serve topped with sliced bananas, fresh berries, or unsweetened almond butter.

To store: Wrap a stack of four pancakes in aluminum foil and place in a resealable plastic bag. To reheat, remove from bag and foil and heat in 30 second intervals in the microwave until warm, or reheat in toaster oven until warm. Pancakes will keep 5 days in the refrigerator and up to 2 months in the freezer.

Chapter 6: Whole Foods Meal Prep Vegetable Recipes

Potato and Cauliflower Mash

Kid-Friendly
7 Ingredients or Less
20 Minutes or Less
Serves 4
Prep Time: 5 minutes
Cook Time: 20 minutes

Ingredients

2 lbs. russet potatoes, peeled and diced into 1-inch pieces
8 oz. cauliflower florets (approximately 1 head)
2 cups chicken broth
1 teaspoon salt
3 tablespoons ghee
1 teaspoon garlic powder

Directions

In a large lidded pot over medium-high heat, add the cauliflower, potatoes, chicken broth, and salt. Bring to a boil, cover, and cook for 20 minutes or until tender. Drain, reserving any excess broth, and return the potatoes and cauliflower to the pot. With a potato masher, immersion blender, or fork, mash to your desired consistency, adding broth as needed for more moisture. Stir in the ghee and garlic powder, and add salt and pepper to taste.

Note: For more flavor, mix in fresh herbs such as thyme or rosemary before serving. You can also stir in ½ cup unsweetened unflavored almond milk for a creamier mash, or use only cauliflower for a lighter mash.

To store: Divide into 4 airtight microwave-safe containers and store in the refrigerator for up to 5 days. Alternatively, add as a side to an already prepped protein main from another chapter. Reheat in microwave in 30-second intervals until warm.

Flavor Bomb Asian Brussels Sprouts

20 Minutes or Less

Serves 4 as a side

Prep Time: 5 minutes

Cook Time: 3 minutes

Ingredients

3 tablespoons soy sauce

3 tablespoons sesame oil

1 tablespoon rice wine vinegar

2 teaspoons garlic powder

1 teaspoon onion powder

1 teaspoon paprika

1/8 teaspoon cayenne pepper

2 tablespoons almonds, chopped, toasted

2 lbs. Brussels sprouts, halved

Directions

Preheat the broiler and place a rack 6 inches from the heat. Line a large baking sheet with aluminum foil or parchment paper.

In a small bowl, combine the soy sauce, sesame oil, rice wine vinegar, garlic powder, onion powder, paprika, cayenne pepper, and salt. Add the halved brussels sprouts and toss.

Bake for 8-12 minutes or until brussels are crispy and tender but still have a bite to them. Top with the toasted almonds and serve warm.

Note: For spicier Brussels sprouts, try doubling or tripling the quantity of cayenne pepper, or add a few tablespoons of your favorite compliant hot sauce.

To store: Divide into 4 airtight microwave-safe containers and store in the refrigerator for up to 5 days. Alternatively, add as a side to an already prepped protein main from another chapter. Reheat in microwave in 30-second intervals until warm.

Instant Pot Sage Spaghetti Squash

20 Minutes or Less
7 Ingredients or Less
Serves 4
Prep Time: 5 minutes
Cook Time: 15 minutes

Ingredients

1 medium spaghetti squash
2 tablespoons olive oil
5 garlic cloves, minced
1 tablespoons fresh sage, chopped
1 teaspoon salt
¼ teaspoon nutmeg
Pepper to taste

Directions

Halve the squash and scoop out any seeds. In the Instant Pot, add 1 cup of water and place the trivet inside. Arrange the two squash halves on the trivet so that the flesh side is facing up. This can either be done side-by-side or stacked on top of each other, depending on the size of your squash and your Instant Pot.

Lock the lid and set the Pressure Release to Sealing. Select the Pressure Cook or Manual setting and set the cooking time to 7 minutes at high pressure.

As the squash pressure cooks, heat the olive oil in a small skillet. Add the garlic, sage, salt, nutmeg, and pepper to taste. Cook until fragrant, 2-4 minutes. Set aside.

Once the timer goes off on the Instant Pot, let sit for at least 10 minutes; the pressure will release naturally. Then switch the Pressure Release to Venting to allow any last steam out.

Remove the squash from the Instant Pot and use a fork to shred the flesh into spaghetti-like strands. Toss with the garlic sage oil, add salt and pepper to taste, and serve warm.

To store: Divide into 4 airtight microwave-safe containers and store in the refrigerator for up to 5 days. Alternatively, add as a side to an already prepped protein main from another chapter. Reheat in microwave in 30-second intervals until warm.

Simplest Balsamic Beets

7 Ingredients or Less
Serves 6 as a side
Prep Time: 1 minute
Cook Time: 10 minutes

Ingredients

6 medium beets, unpeeled
3 tablespoons balsamic vinegar
2 tablespoons olive oil
Salt to taste
Pepper to taste

Oven Directions

Preheat the oven to 400 degrees.

Wash the beets well and remove any leaves. Wrap each beet in aluminum foil and place on a baking sheet. Bake for 35-45 minutes or until tender when pierced with a fork.

Instant Pot Directions

Wash the beets well and remove any leaves. Add 1 cup of water to the Instant Pot and place the trivet on top. Arrange the beets on the trivet.

Lock the lid and set the Pressure Release to Sealing. Select the Pressure Cook or Manual setting and set the cooking time to 10 minutes at high pressure. Once the timer goes off, use a kitchen towel or oven mitts to protect your hand and move the Pressure Release knob to Venting to perform a quick pressure release.

To serve

Allow the beets to cool and peel. The skin should slip off easily. Slice the beets into rounds or chop them into bite-sized pieces. Dress them with the balsamic vinegar, olive oil, and salt and pepper to taste.

Serve immediately or allow to marinate for 30 minutes for more flavor.

To store: Divide into 6 airtight microwave-safe containers and store in the refrigerator for up to 5 days. Alternatively, add as a side to an already prepped protein main from another chapter. Reheat in microwave in 30-second intervals until warm.

Amazingly Adaptable Roasted Rosemary Potatoes

Kid-Friendly

7 Ingredients or Less

20 Minutes or Less

Serves 8

Prep Time: 10 minutes

Cook Time: 20 minutes

Ingredients

1½ lbs. russet potatoes, peeled or unpeeled, in 1-inch pieces

¼ cup olive oil

1 tablespoon fresh rosemary, finely chopped

1 teaspoon garlic powder

1 teaspoon sea salt

Pepper to taste

Directions

Preheat the oven to 450 degrees and line two large baking sheets with aluminum foil or parchment paper.

In a large bowl, toss the potatoes, olive oil, rosemary, salt, garlic powder, and pepper. Spread the potatoes over the two baking sheets, leaving plenty of room between the potatoes.

Roast for 15-20 minutes, or until tender when tested with a fork. Serve warm over a salad or as a side for chicken or another protein.

Note: This recipe can be adapted many ways, according to your family's tastes. Try adding a favorite spice mix, curry powder, or cayenne pepper before roasting, fresh herbs like oregano or thyme after roasting, or a drizzle of truffle oil before serving.

To store: Divide into 8 airtight microwave-safe containers and store in the refrigerator for up to 5 days. Alternatively, add as a side to an already prepped protein main from another chapter. Reheat in microwave in 30-second intervals until warm.

Balsamic and Garlic Stewed Kale

20 Minutes or Less
7 Ingredients or Less
Serves 4 as a side
Prep Time: 5 minutes
Cook Time: 4 minutes

Ingredients

1 tablespoon olive oil
5 cloves garlic, roughly chopped
2 large bunches kale, de-stemmed and roughly chopped
½ cup chicken broth
½ teaspoon salt
Pepper to taste
3 tablespoons balsamic vinegar
Crushed red pepper to taste

Directions

In a large skillet over medium heat, heat the olive oil. Add garlic and cook, stirring constantly, until fragrant, 1-2 minutes. Add the kale in bunches, allowing to wilt as needed to make room for more. Add the broth, salt, and pepper.

Reduce the heat to low and cook until kale is cooked down. Add the balsamic vinegar and crushed red pepper flakes, if using. Taste and add more salt and pepper if necessary. Serve warm.

To store: Divide into 4 airtight microwave-safe containers and store in the refrigerator for up to 5 days. Alternatively, add as a side to an already prepped protein main from another chapter. Reheat in microwave in 30-second intervals until warm.

Butternut Squash and Sage Soup

Kid-Friendly
7 Ingredients or Less
20 Minutes or Less
Serves 4
Prep Time: 10 minutes
Cook Time: 15-20 minutes

Ingredients

1 teaspoon olive oil
1 onion, chopped
4 cloves garlic, minced
1 tablespoon fresh sage, or 1 teaspoon ground sage
3 lb. butternut squash, peeled and cut into 1-inch cubes
3 cups chicken broth
½ teaspoon salt
Pepper to taste
½ cup unsweetened coconut milk
Optional: roasted pumpkin seeds for serving

Directions

In a large stockpot over medium heat, heat olive oil and sauté onion until translucent, about 3 minutes. Add garlic and sage, and cook 1 minute. Add the butternut squash, chicken broth, salt, and pepper, and stir well.

Bring to a boil, reduce heat to medium and simmer uncovered for 15-20 minutes, until squash is soft. Puree in a blender until very smooth, then return to pot. (You can also use an immersion blender for this step.)

Stir in the unsweetened coconut milk and add salt and pepper to taste. Serve topped with roasted pumpkin seeds, if desired.

Notes: For a sweeter soup, add 1 peeled, cored, and diced apple along with the butternut squash.

To store: Allow soup to cool and divide into 8 airtight microwave-safe containers or wide-mouth mason jars. Reheat individually in the microwave in 30-second intervals. Soup will keep up to 5 days in the refrigerator and up to 2 months in the freezer.

Creamiest Broccoli Soup

Kid-Friendly
Serves 8
Prep Time: 10 minutes
Cook Time: 30 minutes

Ingredients

1 tablespoon ghee
½ large onion, diced
3 cloves garlic, minced
4 cups chicken broth
10½ oz. package riced cauliflower, frozen
1½ lbs. broccoli crowns, stems cut into 1-inch chunks, tops cut into ½-inch florets
¼ teaspoon black pepper
Pinch nutmeg
1 tablespoon dried basil
½ teaspoon thyme
1½ cups full-fat coconut milk
Optional: ½ cup toasted walnuts, chopped

Directions

In a large stockpot over medium heat, melt ghee and sauté onion until translucent, about 3 minutes. Add garlic and sauté 1 minute.

Add the chicken broth, riced cauliflower, and broccoli stems. Bring to a boil, reduce heat to medium and simmer uncovered for 15 minutes, until stems are tender. Puree in a blender until very smooth, then return to pot. (You can also use an immersion blender for this step.)

Add the broccoli florets, pepper, nutmeg, basil, thyme, and coconut milk, and stir well. Cover and simmer 10 minutes until florets are tender.

Serve topped with toasted walnuts, if desired.

To store: Allow soup to cool and divide into 8 airtight microwave-safe containers or wide-mouth mason jars. Reheat individually in the microwave in 30-second intervals. Soup will keep up to 5 days in the refrigerator and up to 2 months in the freezer.

6-Ingredient Curried Carrot Soup

20 Minutes or Less

7 Ingredients or Less

Serves 4

Prep Time: 10 minutes

Cook Time: 15 minutes

Ingredients

1 tablespoon ghee

½ yellow onion, chopped

3 cloves garlic, minced

8-10 large carrots, peeled and chopped

1½ cups vegetable broth

1 tablespoon curry powder

1 teaspoon cayenne pepper (optional)

1 teaspoon salt

1 14-oz can unsweetened coconut milk

Stovetop Directions

In a large stockpot over medium heat, melt ghee and sauté onion until translucent, about 3 minutes. Add garlic and sauté 1 minute.

Add carrots, broth, curry powder, cayenne (if using), and salt. Bring to a boil, reduce heat to medium and simmer uncovered for 15-25 minutes, until carrots are tender. Puree in a blender until very smooth, then return to pot. (You can also use an immersion blender.)

Add the coconut milk, and stir well. Taste and add more salt and pepper if needed. Cover and simmer 10 minutes until slightly thickened. Serve warm.

Instant Pot Directions

Select the Sauté setting on the Instant Pot and heat the ghee. Add the onion and garlic and cook, stirring often, until the onion is translucent, 3-5 minutes. Add remaining ingredients, except coconut milk, and stir well.

Press Cancel to reset the cooking method. Lock the lid and set the Pressure Release to Sealing. Select the Pressure Cook or Manual setting and set the cooking time to 15 minutes at high pressure. Once the timer goes off, let sit for at least 10 minutes; the pressure will release naturally. Then switch the Pressure Release to Venting to allow any last steam out.

Open the Instant Pot and puree the soup using an immersion blender or by transferring it to a stand blender. Stir in unsweetened coconut milk, taste, and add more salt and pepper if needed.

To store: Allow soup to cool and divide into 8 airtight microwave-safe containers or wide-mouth mason jars. Reheat individually in the microwave in 30-second intervals. Soup will keep up to 5 days in the refrigerator and up to 2 months in the freezer.

My Signature Lemon Chicken Soup

Kid-Friendly

Serves 4

Prep Time: 10 minutes

Cook Time: 25 minutes

Ingredients

2 tablespoons ghee

1 onion, chopped

3 cloves garlic, minced

2 medium carrots, peeled and sliced

3 stalks celery, sliced

8 cups chicken broth

8 oz. mushrooms, sliced

1 tablespoon fresh thyme, or 1 teaspoon dried thyme

Salt to taste

Pepper to taste

1½ lbs. boneless skinless chicken breasts or thighs

1 bunch kale, stemmed and roughly chopped

2 lemons, juiced

Optional: lemon wedges for serving

Directions

In a large stockpot over medium heat, melt ghee and sauté onion until translucent, about 3 minutes. Add garlic, carrots, and celery, and sauté 2-3 minutes.

Add the chicken broth, mushrooms, and thyme. Taste and add salt and pepper as needed. Add the chicken breasts or thighs and stir well. Bring to a boil, reduce heat to medium and simmer uncovered for 15 minutes, until chicken is cooked through.

Remove the chicken and shred. Add the chicken back to the pot and stir in the kale and lemon juice. Ladle into bowls and serve with an extra squeeze of lemon, drizzle of olive oil, or fresh cracked pepper.

To store: Allow soup to cool and divide into 8 airtight microwave-safe containers or wide-mouth mason jars. Reheat individually in the microwave in 30-second intervals. Soup will keep up to 5 days in the refrigerator and up to 2 months in the freezer.

Instant Pot Fuss-Free French Onion Soup

7 Ingredients or Less

20 Minutes or Less

Serves 4

Prep Time: 5 minutes

Cook Time: 10 minutes

Ingredients

3 tablespoons ghee

3 large onions, halved and then thinly sliced

1 tablespoon balsamic vinegar

2 tablespoons red wine vinegar

6 cups beef or pork broth

2 large sprigs fresh thyme

1 teaspoon salt

Directions

Select the Sauté setting and heat the ghee. Add the onions and stir constantly until completely cooked down and caramelized. This can take 10-20 minutes or more, depending on your onions and the heat of your Instant Pot. If the onions begin to blacken at the edges, use the Adjust button to reduce the heat to Less.

Once the onions have caramelized, add the balsamic vinegar, red wine vinegar, broth, and thyme, and scrape up any browned bits from the bottom of the pot.

Press Cancel to reset the cooking method. Lock the lid and set the Pressure Release to Sealing. Select the Soup setting and set the cooking time to 10 minutes at high pressure.

Once the timer goes off, let sit for at least 10 minutes; the pressure will release naturally. Then switch the Pressure Release to Venting to allow any last steam out. Open the Instant Pot and discard the thyme stems. Season with salt and pepper to taste.

Note: Because this soup is so simple, a good quality broth is essential. I recommend Trader Joe's or Pacific's lines of broth.

To store: Allow soup to cool and divide into 8 airtight microwave-safe containers or wide-mouth mason jars. Reheat individually in the microwave in 30-second intervals. Soup will keep up to 5 days in the refrigerator and up to 2 months in the freezer.

Immune-Boost Chard and Sweet Potato Stew

20 Minutes or Less

Serves 4

Prep Time: 10 minutes

Cook Time: 8 minutes

Ingredients

2 tablespoons olive oil

1 medium onion, diced

1 teaspoon cumin seeds, or 1 teaspoon ground cumin

2 medium sweet potatoes, peeled ½ inch cubes

1 tablespoon fresh ginger, peeled and minced

½ teaspoon turmeric

1 teaspoon ground coriander

1 teaspoon salt

3 cups vegetable broth

1 bunch Swiss chard

Optional: lemon wedges for serving

Directions

In a large stockpot over medium heat, heat the olive oil. Add the onion and cook until translucent, about 3 minutes. If using cumin seeds, add them now and toast them for 1-3 minutes, until fragrant. Otherwise, add the ground cumin in the next step.

Add the sweet potato, ground cumin (if using), ginger, turmeric, coriander, and salt and cook for 3-4 minutes. Add the vegetable broth and chard. Taste and add more salt and pepper if needed.

Bring to a boil, reduce heat to medium and simmer uncovered for 10-15 minutes, until sweet potatoes are tender.

Ladle into bowls and serve warm with a squeeze of lemon juice, if desired.

To store: Allow soup to cool and divide into 8 airtight microwave-safe containers or wide-mouth mason jars. Reheat individually in the microwave in 30-second intervals. Soup will keep up to 5 days in the refrigerator and up to 2 months in the freezer.

The Beefiest Taco Soup

Kid-Friendly

Serves 8

Prep Time: 20 minutes

Cook Time: 15 minutes

Ingredients

1 tablespoon olive oil

2 lbs. ground beef

1 tablespoon cumin

1 tablespoon garlic powder

2 teaspoons chili powder

1 teaspoon dried oregano

1 teaspoon salt

Pepper to taste

½ cup onion, diced

2 (10 oz.) cans diced tomatoes with green chilies

4 cups beef broth

2 avocados, sliced (optional)

Directions

In a large pot over medium-high heat, heat the olive oil. Add the ground beef, cumin, garlic powder, chili powder, oregano, salt, and pepper, and mix well. Continue to brown the beef until it's dark brown, not gray, and any juices dried up, 10-15 minutes. Add the onion and cook 2-3 minutes more, until translucent.

Add the diced tomatoes and beef broth, and scrape up any browned bits from the bottom of the pot. Reduce the heat and simmer for 10-15 minutes. Taste and add more salt and pepper if necessary. Serve warm, topped with sliced avocado if desired

To store: Allow soup to cool and divide into 8 airtight microwave-safe containers or wide-mouth mason jars. Reheat individually in the microwave in 30-second intervals. Soup will keep 5 days in the refrigerator and up to 2 months in the freezer.

Chapter 8: Whole Foods Meal Prep Seafood Recipes

Takeout Asian Salmon & Broccoli

Kid-Friendly

20 Minutes or Less

Serves 4

Prep Time: 5 minutes

Cook Time: 3 minutes

Ingredients:

2 cloves garlic, minced

¼ teaspoon crushed red pepper

½ teaspoon salt

Pepper to taste

3 tablespoons coconut aminos

1 cup chicken broth

4 medium-sized salmon fillets

2 cups broccoli florets

½ lime, juiced

1 tablespoon sesame oil

Directions

In a small bowl, combine half of the minced garlic, crushed red pepper, salt, pepper, and 2 tablespoons of the coconut aminos. Brush the sauce on the salmon fillets.

In a large skillet over medium-high heat, add the salmon fillets and cook, undisturbed, 3-5 minutes until well-seared. Flip the fillets, and lowering the heat to medium, add the broccoli. Cook 4-6 minutes, or until salmon is cooked to desired doneness and broccoli is tender.

Meanwhile, in a small bowl, combine the lime juice, remaining minced garlic, remaining 1 tablespoon of coconut aminos, sesame oil, and salt and pepper to taste. Serve the salmon and broccoli drizzled with the sesame oil sauce.

To store: Divide into 4 airtight microwave-safe containers and store in the refrigerator for up to 5 days or in the freezer for up to 2 months. Reheat in microwave in 30-second intervals until warm.

Light and Fresh Mediterranean Cod

20 Minutes or Less

Serves 4

Prep Time: 1 minute

Cook Time: 20 minutes

Ingredients

1 tablespoon ghee

6 small cod fillets

1 onion, sliced

1-28 oz. can diced tomatoes (no sugar added)

2 tablespoons capers, drained, or 2 tablespoons Kalamata olives, chopped

Juice of 1 lemon

1 teaspoon dried oregano

1 teaspoon salt

Pepper to taste

Directions

In a large skillet over medium-high heat, heat the ghee. Add the cod fillets and cook, undisturbed, 3-5 minutes until well-seared. Flip the fillets, and sear 3-5 minutes on the other side. Remove cod to a plate.

Add onion to the skillet and cook until soft, 3-4 minutes. Add remaining ingredients to the skillet, stir, and cook the sauce for 10-15 minutes, until thickened. Place the cod fillets back in the sauce and spoon sauce over each fillet. Taste the sauce, adding more salt and pepper if necessary.

Serve the cod with the Mediterranean tomato sauce, and if desired, serve over cauliflower rice or mash.

To store: Divide into 4 airtight microwave-safe containers and store in the refrigerator for up to 5 days or in the freezer for up to 2 months. Reheat in microwave in 30-second intervals until warm.

Instant Pot Lemon Garlic Salmon with Green Beans

Kid-Friendly
20 Minutes or Less
7 Ingredients or Less
Serves 4
Prep Time: 5 minutes
Cook Time: 3 minutes

Ingredients:

4 cloves garlic, minced
1 teaspoon salt, divided
Pepper to taste
2 tablespoons ghee, divided
2 tablespoons lemon juice, divided
3 cups green beans, trimmed
4 medium salmon fillets

Directions

In a small bowl, combine half of the minced garlic, ½ teaspoon salt, pepper, and 1 tablespoon each of the ghee and lemon juice. Brush the lemon garlic sauce on the salmon fillets.

In the Instant Pot, add 1 cup water and place the trivet in the bottom of the pot. Arrange the salmon fillets on top of the trivet and top with the green beans. Season green beans lightly with salt and pepper.

Lock the lid and set the Pressure Release to Sealing. Select the Steam setting and set the cooking time to 3 minutes at high pressure. Meanwhile, in a small bowl, combine the remaining minced garlic, remaining 1 tablespoon of ghee, lemon juice, and salt and pepper to taste.

With a kitchen towel or oven mitts protecting your hand, move the Pressure Release knob to Venting to perform a quick pressure release.

Open the lid and taste, adding more salt and pepper if necessary. Serve the salmon and green beans with the lemon garlic sauce.

To store: Divide into 4 airtight microwave-safe containers and store in the refrigerator for up to 5 days or in the freezer for up to 2 months. Reheat in microwave in 30-second intervals until warm.

Spicy Sausage and Kale Mussels

7 Ingredients or Less

Serves 4

1 tablespoon olive oil

1 lb. andouille sausage or spicy Italian sausage (check that it is compliant)

4 cloves garlic, minced

2 (15 oz.) cans diced tomatoes

¼ teaspoon crushed red pepper flakes (or to taste)

1 teaspoon salt

Pepper to taste

2 lbs. mussels

5 cups kale

In a large lidded pot over medium-high heat, heat the olive oil. Add the sausage and cook, stirring often, until browned on all sides and cooked through.

Reduce heat to medium-low and add garlic to the pot. Cook until garlic is fragrant, 1-2 minutes. Add diced tomatoes, red pepper flakes, salt, and pepper, and stir, scraping up any browned bits from the bottom. Add the mussels, cover with lid, and cook until mussels have opened, about 5-7 minutes. Discard any mussels that haven't opened.

Taste the sauce, and add more salt and pepper if necessary. Add the kale in batches, stirring well and allowing it to wilt into the sauce, 3-5 minutes.

Ladle into a bowl and serve with warm, topped with a squeeze of lemon if desired.

To store: Divide into 4 airtight microwave-safe containers and store in the refrigerator for up to 5 days. Reheat in microwave in 30-second intervals until warm.

5-Minute Garlic Citrus Shrimp

Kid-Friendly
20 Minutes or Less
7 Ingredients or Less
Serves 4
Prep Time: 5 minutes
Cook Time: 1 minute

Ingredients

1 tablespoon ghee
4 garlic cloves, minced
½ cup orange juice (100% pure, no sugar added)
½ cup chicken broth
2 pounds of peeled and deveined raw shrimp
2 tablespoons lemon juice
½ teaspoon salt
Pepper to taste

Directions

Select the Sauté setting and heat the ghee. Add the garlic and cook until fragrant, 1-2 minutes. Add the orange juice and chicken broth.

Press Cancel to reset the cooking method, add the shrimp, and season with ½ teaspoon salt. Lock the lid and set the Pressure Release to Sealing. Select the Steam setting and set the cooking time to 1 minute at high pressure.

Once the timer has gone off and with a kitchen towel or oven mitts protecting your hand, move the Pressure Release knob to Venting to perform a quick pressure release.

Open the lid and stir in lemon juice and adjust salt and pepper to taste. Serve over cauliflower rice or mixed vegetables.

To store: Divide into 4 airtight microwave-safe containers and store in the refrigerator for up to 5 days. Reheat in microwave in 30-second intervals until warm.

Chapter 9: Whole Foods Meal Prep Pork Recipes

Pork Dumpling Bowls

Kid-Friendly
Serves 4
Prep Time: 10 minutes
Cook Time: 25 minutes

Ingredients

1½ lbs. ground pork sausage, casings removed (check that it is compliant)
½ medium onion, thinly sliced
1 tablespoon sesame oil
1 head (about 2 pounds) green cabbage, thinly sliced
¼ cup coconut aminos
4 cloves garlic, minced
1 teaspoon dried ground ginger
¼ cup chicken broth
Salt and pepper to taste
3 green onions, sliced
Optional: sriracha or other compliant hot sauce

Directions

In a large skillet over medium-high heat, add the pork sausage, breaking it up into smaller pieces. Allow the pork to sear on one side, undisturbed, then stir and allow to sear again. You want the pork to be dark brown, not gray, and any juices dried up, 10-15 minutes.

Add onion and sesame oil, stir, and allow to cook for 1-2 minutes. Add the cabbage, coconut aminos, garlic, ginger, and chicken broth and stir to combine. Cook for 7-10 minutes, or until cabbage has cooked down. Season, if needed, with salt and pepper and garnish with green onions and sriracha, if desired. Serve warm.

To store: Divide into 4 airtight microwave-safe containers and store in the refrigerator for up to 5 days or in the freezer for up to 2 months. Reheat in microwave in 30-second intervals until warm.

Slow Sunday Pork Ragu

Kid-Friendly
7 Ingredients or Less
Serves 4
Prep Time: 5 minutes
Cook Time: 60-80 minutes

Ingredients

18 oz. pork tenderloin

1 teaspoon salt

Pepper to taste

1 tablespoon olive oil

2 sprigs of fresh thyme, or 2 teaspoons dried thyme

1 teaspoon dried oregano

Optional: 2 bay leaves

6 cloves garlic, whole

1-28 oz. can crushed tomatoes

1 cup chicken broth

Oven Directions

Preheat the oven to 325 degrees. Season pork loin all over with salt and pepper.

In a large lidded dutch oven, heat olive oil over medium-high heat. Add the loin and brown, about 5-7 minutes per side. Add the garlic, crushed tomatoes, chicken broth, thyme, oregano, and bay leaves if using, and scrape up any browned bits from the bottom of the pot.

Cover, and cook in the oven for 60-80 minutes, until tender and falling apart. Remove from oven and taste, adding more salt and pepper if necessary. Shred the pork and serve over spaghetti squash or spoon over vegetable fritters.

Instant Pot Directions

Season the pork loin with salt and pepper. Select the Sauté setting on the Instant Pot and heat the olive oil. Add the pork loin to the Instant Pot and sear on all sides until browned. Add the garlic, crushed tomatoes, thyme, oregano, and if using, bay leaves. Lock the lid and set the Pressure Release to Sealing. Select the Meat/Stew setting and set the cooking time to 45 minutes at high pressure.Once the timer goes off, let sit for at least 10 minutes; the pressure will release naturally. Then switch the Pressure Release to Venting to allow any last steam out. Open the lid and taste, adding more salt and pepper if necessary. Shred the pork and serve over spaghetti squash or spoon over vegetable fritters.

To store: Divide into 4 airtight microwave-safe containers and store in the refrigerator for up to 5 days or in the freezer for up to 2 months. Reheat in microwave in 30-second intervals until warm.

Mushroom Smothered Pork Chops

7 Ingredients or Less
20 Minutes or Less
Serves 4
Prep Time: 5 minutes
Cook Time: 30 minutes

Ingredients

4 ½-inch thick bone-in pork chops (about 5 oz. each)
½ teaspoon paprika
½ teaspoon garlic powder
1 teaspoon salt
Pepper to taste
2 tablespoons ghee
1 medium onion, sliced
6 oz. white mushrooms
2 tablespoons almond flour
½ cup chicken broth

Directions

Preheat the oven to 375 degrees.

Season pork chops with paprika, garlic powder, salt, and pepper. In a large skillet over medium-high heat, heat ghee. Brown the chops on both sides then remove to an oven-safe dish, working in batches of 2 chops at a time if necessary. Set aside the browned chops.

Add onion and mushrooms to skillet and cook about 5 minutes, stirring well. Add almond flour and cook 1-2 minutes more. Add chicken broth, stir, and cook 3-5 minutes more, until slightly reduced. Pour sauce over the pork chops, making sure chops are coated well with sauce. Bake for 20-30 minutes, or until cooked through.

To store: Divide chops and sauce into 4 airtight microwave-safe containers and store in the refrigerator for up to 5 days or in the freezer for up to 2 months. Reheat in the microwave in 30-second intervals until warm.

Ham Salad Stuffed Avocados

20 Minutes or Less

Serves 4

Prep Time: 10 minutes

Cook Time: 0 minutes

Ingredients

24 oz. ham steak or thick-cut ham, cubed (check that it is compliant)

2 stalks celery, finely diced

2 scallions, sliced

4 small pickle spears, finely diced

8 tablespoons mayonnaise (homemade or a compliant brand, such as Sir Kensington's Avocado Oil Mayo)

1 tablespoon whole grain mustard

¼ teaspoon salt

Pepper to taste

4 avocados

Directions

In a medium bowl, combine the ham, celery, scallions, and pickles. Add the mayonnaise, mustard, salt, and pepper and stir until well combined.

Halve the avocados, remove the pit, and spoon the ham salad into the avocado, mounding the salad on top of the avocado. Serve immediately.

To store: Ham salad can be stored in an airtight container in the refrigerator for up to 5 days. Avocados should be halved and pitted right before serving. Serve chilled.

One Pot Artichoke and Lemon Pork Chops

Kid-Friendly
Serves 4
Prep Time: 10 minutes
Cook Time: 3 minutes

Ingredients

3 oz. bacon, diced
4-½ inch thick bone-in pork chops
2 teaspoons ground black pepper
1 shallot, minced
1 teaspoon lemon zest
3 garlic cloves, minced
1 teaspoon dried rosemary
1 cup chicken broth
1 9-oz package frozen artichoke heart quarters

Directions

Preheat the oven to 300 degrees.

In a large lidded dutch oven over medium heat, cook the bacon until it has rendered its fat and turned crispy, about 5 minutes. Transfer to a plate.

Season the pork chops with salt and pepper and add to the skillet. Brown the chops on both sides then remove to a plate, working in batches of 2 chops at a time if necessary.

Add shallots to the skillet and cook for 1 minute. Add lemon zest, garlic, and rosemary and cook until fragrant. Add the chicken broth, artichokes, and cooked bacon. Stir well then nestle the chops back into the sauce and cover the pot.

Cook for 15 minutes, flip the chops and stir the sauce, and cook for 15-25 minutes more, until desired level of tenderness is reached.

Let the chops rest for 10 minutes, then serve with the lemon artichoke sauce.

To store: Divide into 4 airtight microwave-safe containers and store in the refrigerator for up to 5 days or in the freezer for up to 2 months. Reheat in the microwave in 30-second intervals until warm.

Perfect Cuban Pulled Pork

Kid-Friendly

7 Ingredients or Less

Serve: 8

Prep Time: 5 minutes

Cook Time: 2-3 hours

Ingredients

3 lbs. boneless pork shoulder, fat trimmed

6 cloves garlic

2/3 cup grapefruit juice (100% juice, no sugar added)

2 teaspoons fresh oregano, or 1 teaspoon dried oregano

2 teaspoons cumin

1 lime, juiced

1 tablespoon salt

1 bay leaf

Optional for serving: lime wedges, cilantro, salsa, or hot sauce

Directions

Preheat the oven to 325 degrees.

Cut the pork shoulder into 4 evenly sized pieces. In a blender or food processor, combine the garlic, grapefruit juice, oregano, cumin, lime juice, and salt, and blend until combined.

Place the pork shoulder in a large lidded ovenproof pot and coat with the sauce. Cover, and cook in the oven for 2-3 hours, or until tender and falling apart.

Remove from oven and taste, adding more salt and pepper if necessary. Remove the pork, shred, ladle sauce over it, and serve warm.

To store: Divide into 4 airtight microwave-safe containers and store in the refrigerator for up to 5 days or in the freezer for up to 2 months. Reheat in microwave in 30-second intervals until warm.

Italian Sausage and Brussels Bowls

Kid-Friendly

Serves 4

Prep Time: 10 minutes

Cook Time: 20 minutes

Ingredients

1 tablespoon ghee

1½ lbs. sweet Italian sausage

1 lb. brussels sprouts, halved

½ large onion, chopped

½ green bell pepper, chopped

1 cup canned diced tomatoes

1 tablespoon dried basil

1 teaspoon salt

Pepper to taste

Directions

In a large skillet over medium-high heat, heat the ghee and brown the sausage on all sides. Remove the sausage to a plate.

Add brussels sprouts, onion, and bell pepper to the skillet, and sauté about 5-7 minutes, until onion is translucent and brussels are nearly tender. Add diced tomatoes, basil, salt, and pepper, stir well, and cook 5-7 minutes more, until sauce is slightly thickened. Add the sausage back to the skillet, taste, and add more salt and pepper if desired.

Spoon brussels sprouts into a bowl and serve topped with the sausage and the sauce.

To store: Divide into 4 airtight microwave-safe containers and store in the refrigerator for up to 5 days or in the freezer for up to 2 months. Reheat in the microwave in 30-second intervals until warm.

Our Favorite Pulled Pork Carnitas

Kid-Friendly

Serves 6

Prep Time: 7 minutes

Cook Time: 2-3 hours

Ingredients

3 lb. boneless pork shoulder, fat trimmed

2 tablespoons of olive oil

¾ cup chicken or pork broth

1 head butter lettuce

2 carrots, grated

2 limes, cut into wedges

For spice rub:

1 tablespoon cumin

1 tablespoon garlic powder

2 teaspoons salt

2 teaspoons oregano

1 teaspoon pepper

1 teaspoon coriander

½ teaspoon cayenne pepper

Directions

In a large bowl, combine the ingredients for the spice rub. Quarter the pork shoulder in 4 evenly sized pieces and rub all over with the spice rub. Allow the pork to absorb the rub for 30 minutes or up to overnight in the refrigerator.

Preheat the oven to 325 degrees.

In a large lidded ovenproof pot over medium-high heat, heat the olive oil. Add the pork shoulder and sear on all sides until brown, about 4-5 minutes per side. Add chicken or pork broth and scrape up any browned bits at the bottom of the pot.

Cover, and cook in the oven for 2-3 hours, or until tender and falling apart.

Remove from oven and taste, adding more salt and pepper if necessary. Shred the pork shoulder and serve in butter lettuce cups, topped with grated carrot and lime juice.

To store: Divide into 4 airtight microwave-safe containers and store in the refrigerator for up to 5 days or in the freezer for up to 2 months. Reheat in microwave in 30-second intervals until warm.

Chapter 10: Whole Foods Meal Prep Beef Recipes

Fajita Stuffed Baked Potatoes

Kid-Friendly
Prep Time: 15 Minutes
Cook Time: 20 minutes
4 medium potatoes
2 tablespoons olive oil, divided
1 ½ lbs. skirt steak, sliced
2 green bell peppers, seeded and sliced
1 red bell pepper, seeded and sliced
1 large onion, sliced
½ cup beef broth
Optional: lime wedges for serving
For fajita seasoning:
1 tablespoon cumin
2 teaspoons chili powder
2 teaspoons garlic powder
1 teaspoon dried oregano
1 teaspoon salt
½ teaspoon black pepper
¼ teaspoon cayenne pepper, or to taste

Preheat the oven to 425 degrees. Prick the potatoes all over with a fork to allow steam to vent and wrap in aluminum foil. Bake for 40-50 minutes, until soft.

Meanwhile, in a small bowl, combine the fajita seasoning ingredients.

In a large skillet over medium-high heat, heat 1 tablespoon of the olive oil. Add half of the steak and sear on all sides. Remove to a plate and sear the second half of the steak. Remove to a plate again. Add the remaining 1 tablespoon of olive oil to skillet, then add the onion and bell peppers. Cook undisturbed until seared on one side, then toss and sear again, until cooked down, 10-12 minutes.

Add the beef broth and scrape up any browned bits from the bottom of the skillet. Add the steak and spice mix and stir well. Allow to cook for 2-4 minutes, until broth has mostly evaporated.

Cut a slit in the baked potatoes, scoop out some of the insides, and stuff with the steak and vegetable fajitas. Serve with a squeeze of lime or guacamole.

To store: Divide into 4 airtight microwave-safe containers and store in the refrigerator for up to 5 days. Reheat in microwave in 30-second intervals until warm.

Sheet Pan Cajun Steak and Brussels Sprouts

20 Minutes or Less
Serves 4
Prep Time: 15 minutes
Cook Time: 5 minutes

Ingredients

1 lb. brussels sprouts, halved
1 large red onion, quartered
3 tablespoons olive oil, divided
1 teaspoon salt, divided
1½ lbs. flat iron steak
1 teaspoon garlic powder
½ teaspoon paprika
½ teaspoon chili powder
½ teaspoon dried thyme
½ teaspoon dried oregano
¼ teaspoon cayenne pepper (or to taste)
Pepper to taste

Directions

Preheat the broiler and place a rack about 6 inches from the heat.

On a large baking sheet, toss the brussels sprouts and onion in 2 tablespoons of the olive oil and season with ½ teaspoon of the salt. Place the flat iron steak in the center of the baking sheet and rub on both sides with remaining 1 tablespoon olive oil and the remaining salt, garlic powder, paprika, chili powder, thyme, oregano, cayenne pepper, and pepper.

Broil for 10 minutes, then flip the steak and broil for 2-4 minutes more, to desired level of doneness. Let rest for 3-4 minutes, then slice steak and serve over the brussels sprouts and onions.

To store: Divide into 4 airtight microwave-safe containers and store in the refrigerator for up to 5 days. Reheat in microwave in 30-second intervals until warm.

Rosemary Braised Beef Short Ribs

7 Ingredients or Less

Serves 5

Prep Time: 10 minutes

Cook Time: 2-3 hours

Ingredients

4 lbs. beef short ribs

1 teaspoon salt

1 tablespoon olive oil

1 medium onion, quartered

6 cloves garlic, minced

¼ cup red wine vinegar

1½ cup beef broth

1 tablespoon fresh rosemary, or 1 ½ teaspoons dried rosemary

Directions

Preheat the oven to 325 degrees.

Season short ribs all over with salt. In a large lidded ovenproof skillet, heat the olive oil. Brown the ribs on all sides, working in batches if necessary.

Add onion, garlic, red wine vinegar, beef broth, and rosemary, turning the ribs to coat them well. Cover, and cook in the oven for 2-3 hours, or until tender and falling apart.

Remove from oven and taste, adding more salt and pepper if necessary. Remove the ribs and spoon the sauce over them. Serve over cauliflower rice or roasted brussels sprouts, if desired.

To store: Divide into 4 airtight microwave-safe containers and store in the refrigerator for up to 5 days or in the freezer for up to 2 months. Reheat in microwave in 30-second intervals until warm.

Burrito Bowl Lettuce Cups

Kid-Friendly
Serves 4
Prep Time: 10 minutes
Cook Time: 5 minutes

Ingredients

2 tablespoons olive oil, divided
1 lb. ground beef
1 tablespoon cumin
2 teaspoons chili powder
2 teaspoons garlic powder
1 teaspoon oregano
1 ½ teaspoons salt
Pepper to taste
½ red or green bell pepper, diced
½ red onion, diced
½ cup beef broth
1 tablespoon lime juice
1 head butter lettuce, separated into lettuce cups
Optional: hot sauce, green onions, sliced avocado, lime wedges

Directions

In a large skillet over medium-high heat, heat the olive oil. Add the ground beef, cumin, chili powder, garlic powder, oregano, salt, and pepper and stir well. Brown the beef until it's seared to a dark brown, not gray, and any juices dried up, 10-15 minutes. Remove to a plate.

In the same skillet, heat the remaining 1 tablespoon of olive oil. Add the bell pepper and onion and cook, undisturbed, until seared on one side. Stir, then allow to cook once more undisturbed, until nicely seared.

Add the beef broth and stir well, scraping up any browned bits from the bottom of the skillet. Add the ground beef back to the skillet and allow to cook until liquid has mostly dried up. Remove from heat, add the lime juice, and taste, adding more salt and pepper if necessary. Scoop into lettuce cups and serve with your favorite toppings.

To store: Divide filling into 4 airtight microwave-safe containers and store in the refrigerator for up to 5 days or in the freezer for up to 2 months. Reheat in microwave in 30-second intervals until warm. Keep butter lettuce cups and toppings separate until serving.

Instant Pot Simplest Beef Stroganoff

Kid-Friendly

20 Minutes or Less

Serves 4

Prep Time: 10 minutes

Cook Time: 18 minutes

Ingredients

1 tablespoon almond flour

1 teaspoon salt

¼ teaspoon pepper

1 lb. beef stew meat, cut into strips

1 tablespoon olive oil

1 onion, chopped

3 cloves garlic, minced

1 cup mushrooms, sliced

2 tablespoons tomato paste

3 tablespoons red wine vinegar

2 cups beef broth

Directions

In a large bowl, mix the almond flour, salt, and pepper. Add the beef strips and toss to coat well.

Select the Sauté setting on the Instant Pot and heat the olive oil. Shake any excess flour from the beef and sauté until well-browned. Add the remaining ingredients to the Instant Pot.

Press Cancel to reset the cooking method. Lock the lid and set the Pressure Release to Sealing. Select the Meat/Stew setting and set the cooking time to 18 minutes at medium pressure.

Once the timer goes off, let sit for at least 10 minutes; the pressure will release naturally. Then switch the Pressure Release to Venting to allow any last steam out. Open the lid and taste, adding more salt and pepper if necessary. Serve with zucchini noodles or roasted potatoes.

To store: Divide into 4 airtight microwave-safe containers and store in the refrigerator for up to 5 days or in the freezer for up to 2 months. Reheat in microwave in 30-second intervals until warm. If serving with zoodles, keep separate until ready to serve.

Best Bacon-Wrapped Meatloaf

Kid-Friendly

Serves 8

Prep Time: 15 minutes

Cook Time: 60 minutes

Ingredients

1 tablespoon olive oil

½ large onion, diced

3 cloves garlic, minced

1 pound ground beef

1 pound ground pork

1 tablespoon oregano

1 tablespoon coconut aminos

2 eggs

1 (12 oz.) package bacon

Glaze

4 tablespoons tomato sauce

½ teaspoon garlic powder

½ teaspoon chili powder

½ teaspoon coconut aminos

½ teaspoon liquid smoke

1 tablespoon apple cider vinegar

Directions

Preheat oven to 400 degrees and spray a 9"x13" baking dish with cooking spray. Line a 9"x5" loaf pan with the bacon, slightly overlapping the strips.

In a large skillet over medium heat, heat the olive oil. Add onion and cook for 3 minutes. Add the garlic and cook for 1 more minute. Remove from heat and set aside.

In a large bowl, mix the beef, pork, oregano, coconut aminos, sautéed onions and garlic, and eggs. In a small bowl, mix the glaze ingredients. Pour glaze over the bacon in the loaf pan. Press the ground meat into the loaf pan. Wrap the ends of the bacon slices over the meat mixture. Flip the loaf pan onto the baking pan and tuck any loose ends of bacon under the meatloaf.

Bake for 1 hour. Bacon should be crispy and fat rendered, and the internal temperature should be 155 degrees. Let meatloaf rest for 10 minutes before slicing.

To store: Slice meatloaf and portion into 8 airtight microwave-safe containers and store in the refrigerator for up to 5 days or in the freezer for up to 2 months. Reheat in microwave in 30-second intervals until warm.

Lone Star State Beef Chili

Kid-Friendly

Serves 4

Prep Time: 10 minutes

Cook Time: 35 minutes

Ingredients

1 tablespoon olive oil

1 lb. ground beef

1 green bell pepper, seeded and diced

1 large onion, chopped

1 medium carrot, finely diced

¼ teaspoon black pepper

1 teaspoon salt

1 teaspoon onion powder

1 tablespoon lime juice

1 tablespoon chili powder

1 teaspoon paprika

2 teaspoons garlic powder

2 teaspoons cumin

2-14 oz. cans fire roasted tomatoes

Directions

In a large pot over medium heat, heat the olive oil. Add the ground beef and brown until it's seared to a dark brown, not gray, and any juices dried up, 10-15 minutes. Add all remaining ingredients and stir well, scraping up any browned bits from the bottom of the pot. Bring to a boil, reduce heat to medium, and simmer uncovered for 20-30 minutes, stirring occasionally and until slightly thickened.

Taste and add more salt and pepper if desired, or a compliant hot sauce if desired. Serve over cauliflower steaks or baked potatoes, or ladle into a bowl and top with guacamole.

To store: Allow chili to cool and divide into 4 airtight microwave-safe containers or wide-mouth mason jars. Reheat individually in the microwave in 30-second intervals. Chili will keep up to 5 days in the refrigerator and up to 2 months in the freezer.

Totally Compliant Sloppy Joes

Kid-Friendly
20 Minutes or Less
Serves 4
Prep Time: 10 minutes
Cook Time: 10 minutes

Ingredients

1 tablespoon ghee
1 lb. ground beef
1 teaspoon salt
Pepper to taste
1 green or red bell pepper, finely chopped
1 onion, finely chopped
3 cloves garlic, minced
1 (14 oz.) can tomato sauce
1 tablespoon apple cider vinegar
1 tablespoon Dijon mustard

Directions

In a medium skillet over medium-high heat, heat the ghee. Add the ground beef, salt, and pepper and cook until seared to a dark brown, not gray, and any juices dried up, 10-15 minutes.

Add the bell pepper, onion, and garlic and cook 4-6 minutes, until softened. Add the tomato sauce, vinegar, and mustard. Cook for 10-15 minutes, until thickened but still loose.

Taste and add salt and pepper if necessary. Serve over cauliflower steaks or as the filling to a baked potato.

Note: These Sloppy Joes will be less sweet than you might be used to, because they don't rely on sugar-packed ketchup. To add more sweetness, you can puree 5 pitted dates in a food processor with a bit of water and incorporate into the sauce before pressure cooking.

To store: Divide into 4 airtight microwave-safe containers and store in the refrigerator for up to 5 days or in the freezer for up to 2 months. Reheat in microwave in 30-second intervals until warm.

Cumin-Spiced Pulled Beef Carnitas

Kid-Friendly

Serves 8   Cook Time: 1½-2 hours

Prep Time: 10 minutes

Ingredients

3 lbs. boneless beef chuck roast, larger pieces of fat trimmed

1 tablespoon olive oil

1 cup beef broth, plus more

½ small green cabbage, shredded

5 tablespoons mayonnaise (homemade or a compliant brand, such as Sir Kensington's Avocado Oil Mayo)

1 tablespoon apple cider vinegar

2 teaspoons mustard (check that it is compliant)

1 head butter lettuce

For spice rub:

1 tablespoon cumin	2 teaspoons oregano
1 tablespoon garlic powder	½ teaspoon pepper
2 teaspoons salt	¼ teaspoon cayenne pepper

Directions

Preheat the oven to 325 degrees. In a large bowl, combine the ingredients for the spice rub. Quarter the roast into 4 evenly sized pieces and rub all over with the spice rub.

In a large lidded ovenproof pot over medium-high heat, heat the olive oil. Add the roast and sear on all sides until brown, about 4-5 minutes per side. Add beef broth and scrape up any browned bits at the bottom of the pot.

Cover, and cook in the oven for 1½-2 hours, or until tender and falling apart. Check occasionally, and if drying out, add more broth.

Meanwhile, combine cabbage, mayonnaise, mustard, apple cider vinegar, salt, and pepper to taste. Set aside

Remove roast from the oven and taste, adding more salt and pepper if necessary. Shred and allow to soak up any sauce. Serve in butter lettuce cups topped with the slaw.

To store: Divide beef into 4 airtight microwave-safe containers and store in the refrigerator for up to 5 days or in the freezer for up to 2 months. Reheat in microwave in 30-second intervals until warm. Keep slaw and butter lettuce cups separate until serving.

Chapter 11: Whole Foods Meal Prep Chicken Recipes

Lemon Butter Chicken Thighs

Kid-Friendly

7 Ingredients or Less

20 Minutes or Less

Serves 4

Prep Time: 1 minute

Cook Time: 20 minutes

Ingredients

1 pound boneless chicken thighs

½ teaspoon salt

¼ teaspoon pepper

3 tablespoons ghee (clarified butter)

4 cloves garlic, minced

1 lemon, zested and sliced into ¼ inch slices, seeds removed

2 teaspoons dried Italian herb mix (or Italian Seasoning found in Seasoning section of this book)

½ cup chicken broth

1 bunch fresh parsley, chopped

Directions

Pat the thighs dry and season with salt and pepper. Melt ghee in a medium skillet over medium-high heat. Add chicken skin side down and let crisp without moving, 8-10 minutes. Flip and lower heat to medium to allow crisping on second side, 3-5 minutes.

Add garlic and stir for about 30 seconds, until fragrant. Add lemon zest, lemon slices, Italian herb mix, and broth. Let chicken simmer for 2-4 minutes or until cooked through.

Remove chicken and lemon slices from skillet and keep warm. Add parsley to sauce in the skillet and mix well. Serve thighs drizzled with the lemon butter sauce.

To store: Divide thighs into 4 servings in individual airtight microwave-safe containers. Reheat in the microwave in 30 second intervals until warm. Thighs can be stored in the refrigerator for up to 5 days and in the freezer for up to 2 months.

Easy Thyme Chicken and Potatoes

Kid-Friendly

20 Minutes or Less

Serves 4

Prep Time: 10 minutes

Cook Time: 15-20 minutes

Ingredients

2 lbs. boneless skinless chicken breasts

1 ½ teaspoons salt, divided

1 tablespoon olive oil

2 cups chicken broth

2 cloves garlic, minced

1 cup pearl onions (can be frozen), or 1 medium onion, sliced

2 cups carrots, diced

1½ lbs. small potatoes, cut in 1-inch pieces

1 sprig fresh rosemary, or 1 teaspoon dried rosemary

1 sprig fresh thyme, or 1 teaspoon dried thyme

Pepper to taste

Directions

Season the chicken breasts on both sides with ½ teaspoon of the salt. Heat olive oil in a deep lidded skillet over medium-high heat. Brown the chicken breasts, about 5 minutes per side.

Add the chicken broth and scrape up any browned bits from the bottom of the pot. Add the garlic, onion, carrots, and potatoes. Sprinkle the potatoes with rosemary, thyme, and the remaining 1 teaspoon salt. Stir well.

Cover the skillet and reduce heat to medium low. Keep covered and simmer until potatoes are cooked through, about 15-20 minutes. If needed, add more broth to keep chicken and potatoes moist.

Open the lid, taste, and add more salt, pepper, rosemary, or thyme if desired. Serve in bowls with the broth.

To store: Divide into 4 servings in individual airtight microwave-safe containers. Reheat in the microwave in 30 second intervals until warm. Can be stored in the refrigerator for up to 5 days and in the freezer for up to 2 months.

Game-Time Buffalo Wings and Buffalo Cauliflower

Kid-Friendly
7 Ingredients or Less
Serves 4
Prep Time: 1 minute
Cook Time: 45 minutes

Ingredients

½ cup Frank's Red Hot Sauce, divided
5 tablespoons ghee
2 lbs. chicken wings
5 cups cauliflower florets

Directions

Preheat oven to 400 degrees. In a medium bowl, whisk together the Frank's Red Hot Sauce and ghee. In a large bowl, toss the chicken wings in half of the buffalo sauce and use a second large bowl to toss the cauliflower florets in the remaining sauce.

Spread the wings on 3 baking sheets, leaving plenty of space between the wings. Bake for 30 minutes, then add the cauliflower to the trays, sprinkling the florets among the chicken. Bake for an additional 10 minutes.

Optional: For crispier wings and cauliflower, set under the broiler until they reach your desired level of crispiness.

To store: Divide wings and cauliflower into 4 servings in individual airtight microwave-safe containers. Reheat in the microwave in 30 second intervals until warm, or reheat in a 350 degree oven until warm. Wings can be stored in the refrigerator for up to 5 days and in the freezer for up to 2 months.

Pesto Chicken, Spinach, and Cauliflower Bowls

Kid-Friendly
7 Ingredients or Less
Serves 4
Prep Time: 10 minutes
Cook Time: 20 minutes

Ingredients

1 tablespoon ghee
1 ½ pounds boneless skinless chicken breasts
1 teaspoon salt
Pepper to taste
1 head cauliflower, chopped into 1-inch florets
½ cup chicken stock
4 cups fresh spinach
½ cup pine nuts or walnuts, toasted
3 cups fresh basil leaves
3 cloves garlic
1 ½ cups olive oil

Directions

In a large skillet, heat 1 tablespoon ghee over medium-high heat. Add chicken and season with salt and pepper, cooking both sides until browned, about 8-10 minutes. Add the cauliflower and cook another 5-7 minutes, until tender but not too soft. Add the chicken stock and scrape any browned bits from the bottom of the skillet. Add the spinach in batches, allowing to wilt, and let any liquid cook down, until mostly dissolved. Remove from heat.

Meanwhile, in a food processor, combine nuts, basil, garlic, and olive oil. Pulse until smoothly combined. Add salt and pepper to taste.

Place chicken in bowls, top with cauliflower and spinach, and drizzle with pesto. Serve warm, drizzled with additional olive oil or a squeeze of lemon juice, if desired.

To store: Divide into 4 servings in individual airtight microwave-safe containers. Reheat in the microwave in 30 second intervals until warm. Can be stored in the refrigerator for up to 5 days and in the freezer for up to 2 months.

Fiesta Pulled Chicken Lettuce Tacos

Kid-Friendly
7 Ingredients or Less
Serves 4
Prep Time: 5 minutes
Cook Time: 20 minutes

Ingredients

2 pounds boneless skinless chicken breasts or thighs
1 tablespoon chili powder
2 teaspoons ground cumin
1 teaspoon garlic powder
1 teaspoon oregano
1 teaspoon salt
1 tablespoon olive oil
1 cup low-sodium chicken broth
1 head butter lettuce, separated into lettuce cups
Optional: sliced green onion, sliced avocado, fresh cilantro, hot sauce

Oven Directions

Preheat the oven to 325 degrees. Season chicken on both sides with chili powder, cumin, garlic powder, oregano, and salt.

In a large lidded dutch oven, heat olive oil over medium-high heat. Add the chicken and brown, about 5-7 minutes per side. Add the chicken broth and scrape up any browned bits from the bottom of the pot. Cover, and braise in the oven for 60-90 minutes, adding more broth if needed to keep the chicken moist. Once tender, shred the chicken, taste, and add salt and pepper if needed. Allow each person to assemble their own lettuce taco with any desired toppings.

Instant Pot Directions

Season chicken on both sides with chili powder, cumin, garlic powder, oregano, and salt. Select the Sauté setting on the Instant Pot and heat the olive oil. Brown the chicken, about 5 minutes per side. Add the chicken broth and scrape up any browned bits from the bottom of the pot.

Press Cancel to reset the cooking method. Lock the lid and set the Pressure Release to Sealing. Select the Poultry setting and set the cooking time to 10 minutes at high pressure. Once the timer goes off, let sit for at least 10 minutes; the pressure will release naturally. Then switch the Pressure Release to Venting to allow any last steam out.

Open the lid and taste, adding more salt and pepper if necessary. Shred the chicken, and allow each person to assemble their own lettuce taco with any desired toppings.

To store: Divide chicken into 4 airtight microwave-safe containers and store in the refrigerator for up to 5 days or in the freezer for up to 2 months. Reheat in microwave in 30-second intervals until warm. Keep butter lettuce cups and toppings separate until serving.

Genovese Chicken Zoodle Bowls

Kid-Friendly

Serves 4

Prep Time: 40 minutes

Cook Time: 2 minutes

Ingredients

2 large zucchini

1 cup grape tomatoes

4 tablespoons olive oil, divided

1 lb. boneless chicken thighs

½ teaspoon dried oregano

½ teaspoon salt

¼ teaspoon pepper

5 cloves garlic, minced

12 oz. genoa salami, sliced

Optional: 1 tablespoon fresh basil, torn

Directions

Spiralize the zucchini on the thickest setting and halve the tomatoes.

Heat 2 tablespoons olive oil in a large skillet over medium-high heat. Season the chicken on both sides with oregano, salt, and pepper, place in the skillet skin side down, and sear for 6-8 minutes without moving. Flip and cook an additional 4-5 minutes, or until cooked through. Chop into 1-inch cubes and set aside.

Reduce heat to medium and add the remaining 2 tablespoons olive oil and garlic to the skillet. Cook until golden, about 30 seconds. Add the tomatoes. Reduce heat to low and cook until tomatoes soften, about 15 minutes.

Meanwhile, chop the salami into ½-inch pieces. Increase the heat to high and add cooked chicken, zucchini, and salami to skillet. Toss and cook for two minutes until combined and season to taste with salt and pepper. Serve warm.

To store: Divide into 4 airtight microwave-safe containers and store in the refrigerator for up to 5 days. Reheat in microwave in 30-second intervals until warm.

Better-Than-Store-Bought Rotisserie Chicken

Kid-Friendly
7 Ingredients or Less
Serves 6
Prep Time: 15 minutes
Cook Time: 20 minutes

Ingredients

1 4-5 pound whole chicken
2 ½ teaspoons kosher salt
2 teaspoons freshly ground pepper
1 teaspoon dried thyme, or 1 tablespoon fresh thyme, chopped
1 lemon, cut in wedges

Directions

Preheat the oven to 450 degrees.

Pat the chicken dry with paper towels. You want the chicken to be as dry as possible. Rub the chicken all over with salt, pepper, and thyme.

Place chicken, breast side up, in a large baking pan and roast for 50-70 minutes, until a thermometer inserted into the thickest part of the thigh reads 165 degrees. Transfer to a platter, and let sit for 5-7 minutes before carving. Serve warm, with a lemon wedge for squeezing over.

To store: Divide chicken into 6 airtight microwave-safe containers and store in the refrigerator for up to 5 days or in the freezer for up to 2 months. Reheat in microwave in 30-second intervals until warm.

Easiest Chicken Curry

4

Prep Time: 10 minutes

Cook Time: 20-30 minutes

Ingredients

1 tablespoon ghee

1½ large yellow onion, chopped

1 teaspoon salt

2 teaspoons garlic powder

2 teaspoons ground ginger

2 heaping teaspoons turmeric

¼ teaspoon cayenne powder

2 teaspoons paprika

2 teaspoons garam masala

1-16-oz can stewed tomatoes, partially drained

1/2 cup tomato paste

2-14 oz. cans unsweetened coconut milk

2 lbs. boneless skinless chicken breasts or thighs

Directions

In a large lidded pot over medium heat, heat the ghee. Add the onion and cook until translucent, about 3-5 minutes. Add the salt, garlic powder, ground ginger, turmeric, cayenne, paprika, and garam masala, and sauté for 2 minutes. Add the canned tomatoes, tomato paste, and unsweetened coconut milk and mix well. Add the chicken breasts or thighs and stir to coat in the sauce.

Bring to a boil, then reduce heat to medium and simmer, covered, for 20-30 minutes, or until chicken is cooked through and tender.

Open the lid and taste, adding more salt and pepper if necessary. Break the chicken into smaller pieces but don't fully shred it. Serve with zoodles or cucumber noodles.

To store: Divide chicken into 4 airtight microwave-safe containers and store in the refrigerator for up to 5 days or in the freezer for up to 2 months. Reheat in microwave in 30-second intervals until warm. If serving with spiralized vegetables, keep them separate until serving.

Our Go-To BBQ Drumsticks

Kid-Friendly
20 Minutes or Less
7 Ingredients or Less
Serves 4
Prep Time: 10-20 minutes
Cook Time: 25-35 minutes

Ingredients

½ cup unsweetened apple juice
¼ cup tomato paste
1 teaspoon garlic powder
1 teaspoon onion powder
1 teaspoon paprika
¼ teaspoon cayenne pepper (Or ½ teaspoon, if you like spicy BBQ sauce.)
1 teaspoon salt
2 tablespoons apple cider vinegar
Optional: 1 teaspoon liquid smoke
12 chicken drumsticks

Directions

Preheat the oven to 425 degrees. Line a baking sheet with aluminum foil and brush with olive oil or ghee.

In a small saucepan over medium-low heat, add all of the ingredients except the drumsticks and stir well. Allow to cook for at least 10 minutes and up to 20 minutes, until thickened. Taste and adjust salt or spice level to your taste. Set aside ¼ of the sauce to brush on at the end.

Arrange the drumsticks on the baking sheet and brush with the BBQ sauce. Bake for 25-35 minutes, until cooked through. Brush with remaining sauce and serve warm.

Optional: For crispier, more charred drumsticks, set the drumsticks under the broiler for 1-3 minutes, until they reach your desired level of char.

Note: This barbeque sauce will be less sweet than you might be used to, because it has no added sugar. To add more sweetness, you can puree 5 pitted dates in a food processor with a bit of water and incorporate into the sauce. Or, if you're in a pinch, you can always use a high-quality Whole Foods compliant sauce.

To store: Divide into 4 airtight microwave-safe containers and store in the refrigerator for up to 5 days or in the freezer for up to 2 months. Reheat in microwave in 30-second intervals until warm.

Metric Conversion Charts

If you use metric measurements in your cooking, use these handy charts to convert the recipes in this book to work in your kitchen. You can also find free and easy-to-use metric conversion calculators online.

1/4 tsp	= 1 ml		
1/2 tsp	= 2 ml		
1 tsp	= 5 ml		
3 tsp	= 1 tbl	= 1/2 fl oz	= 15 ml
2 tbls	= 1/8 cup	= 1 fl oz	= 30 ml
4 tbls	= 1/4 cup	= 2 fl oz	= 60 ml
5 1/3 tbls	= 1/3 cup	= 3 fl oz	= 80 ml
8 tbls	= 1/2 cup	= 4 fl oz	= 120 ml
10 2/3	= 2/3 cup	= 5 fl oz	= 160 ml
12 tbls	= 3/4 cup	= 6 fl oz	= 180 ml
16 tbls	= 1 cup	= 8 fl oz	= 240 ml
1 pt	= 2 cups	= 16 fl oz	= 480 ml
1 qt	= 4 cups	= 32 fl oz	= 960 ml
		33 fl oz	= 1000ml = 1 l

Freeze Water	32° F	0° C	
Room Temp.	68° F	20° C	
Boil Water	212° F	100° C	
Bake	325° F	160° C	3
	350° F	180° C	4
	375° F	190° C	5
	400° F	200° C	6
	425° F	220° C	7
	450° F	230° C	8

CPSIA information can be obtained
at www.ICGtesting.com
Printed in the USA
BVHW011427170622
640069BV00011B/263

9 781913 982126